Table of Contents

Study Hints

The Project Scope Management questions on the PMP® certification exam cover a diverse, yet fundamental, set of project management topics. Project planning, work breakdown structures, project life cycle, project charter, project selection methods, scope statement, scope verification, scope management plan, and scope changes are among the topics covered.

PMI® views Project Scope Management as a five-step process that consists of scope planning, scope definition, WBS creation, scope verification, and scope control. PMBOK® Figure 5-1 provides an overview of this structure. Know this chart thoroughly.

The Project Scope Management questions on the exam are straightforward. Historically, most people have found them to be relatively easy; however, do not be lulled into a false sense of security by past results. These questions cover a wide breadth of material, and you must be familiar with the terminology and perspectives adopted by PMI®.

Following is a list of the major Project Scope Management topics. Use it to help focus your study efforts on the areas most likely to appear on the exam.

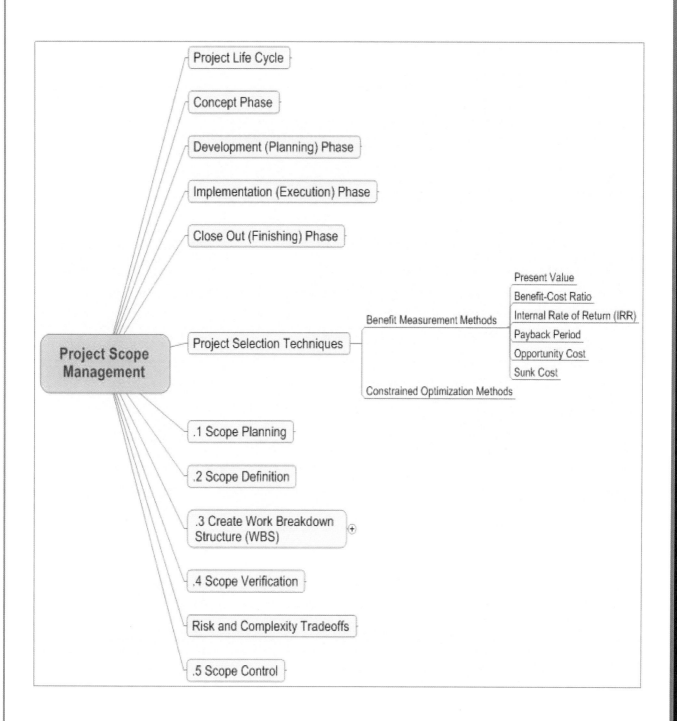

Project Life Cycle

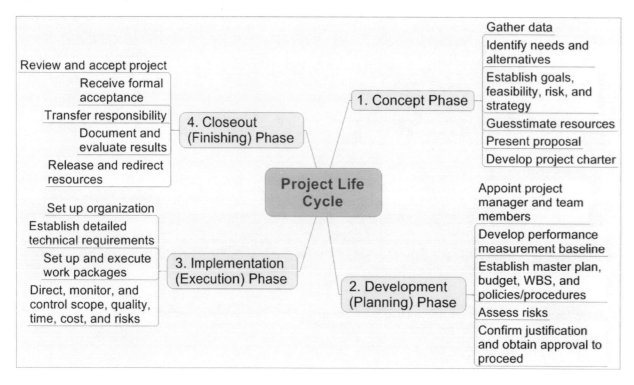

Numerous questions may appear on the test relating to the project life cycle. PMI® states that the project life cycle defines the beginning and end of the project (PMBOK® Para. 2.1.1), describes the technical work to be done in each phase, and identifies who should be involved. Life-cycle descriptions may be general or detailed with the more detailed approaches often called project management methodologies. Most life-cycle descriptions share these common characteristics:

- Cost and staffing levels are low at the start of the project, higher toward the end, and then drop off when the project comes to an end.

- The probability of successfully completing the project is low at the start because uncertainty is high. The probability of successful completion gets progressively higher as the project continues and work is completed. Therefore, there is always a higher degree of risk at the beginning of any project.

- The ability of stakeholders to influence the final characteristics of the project's product and final cost is highest at the start and then gets progressively lower as the project continues. This is because the cost of changes and error correction increases geometrically as the project nears completion. This fact underscores the importance of gathering accurate requirements at the beginning of a project.

Know the four phases of the life cycle and be able to identify activities associated with each life-cycle phase. PMI® recognizes a variety of possible project life cycles (PMBOK® Para. 2.1.3). However, the life cycle tested on the exam usually consists of the following four phases and associated activities:

Concept Phase

- Gather data
- Identify needs and alternatives
- Establish goals, feasibility, risk, and strategy
- Guesstimate resources
- Present proposal
- Develop project charter

Development (Planning) Phase

- Appoint project manager and key team members
- Develop performance measurement baseline
- Establish master plan, budget, WBS, and policies/procedures
- Assess risks
- Confirm justification and obtain approval to proceed

Implementation (Execution) Phase

- Set up organization
- Establish detailed technical requirements
- Set up and execute work packages
- Direct, monitor, and control scope, quality, time, cost, and risks

Closeout (Finishing) Phase

- Review and accept project
- Receive formal acceptance
- Transfer responsibility
- Document and evaluate results
- Release and redirect resources

Project Selection Techniques

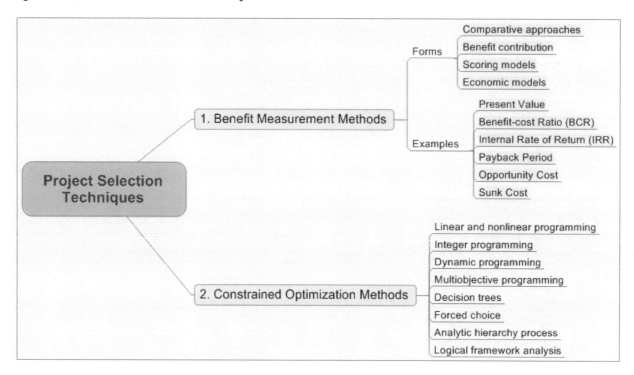

Be familiar with common project selection techniques, which involve measuring value to the project owner. Techniques include considering the decision criterion and calculating value under uncertainty-the decision method and the calculation method. Project selection also applies to choosing alternative ways to complete the project. Two categories of selection techniques are identified: benefit measurement methods and constrained optimization methods.

Benefit Measurement Methods

- Comparative approaches
- Benefit contribution
- Scoring models
- Economic models

Following are specific examples of benefit measurement methods that may appear on the exam.

Present Value

Present value is defined as the value in current monetary units of work to be performed in the future. It is determined by discounting the future price of work by a rate (discount rate) commensurate with the interest rate on the funds for the period before payment is required. In simple terms, present value is the value today of future cash flows. Although we have observed a decrease in the number of present value questions on the exam, you should be knowledgeable of the concept.

Benefit-cost Ratio (BCR)

Benefit-cost analysis results in the calculation of a benefit-cost ratio. This provides a measure of the expected profitability of a project by dividing expected revenues by expected costs. Although some managers prefer relatively simple and straightforward measures of benefits and costs, in practice, the measures of the benefits and the costs are sometimes modified to consider more complex trade-offs. However, the exam does not test the exact formulas, focusing instead on the concept. You should know the following:

- A BCR of 1.0 means that expected benefits and costs are equal, that is, you have a break-even project.

- A BCR less than 1.0 means that costs are expected to exceed benefits, that is, the project is not financially attractive.

- A BCR greater than 1.0 is a profitable project The higher the ratio, the better the project For example, a BCR of 2.5 means that you expect a gross payback of $2.50 for every dollar expended on the project

Internal Rate of Return (IRR)

IRR is another quantitative measure of a project's expected profitability. IRR can be thought of as the average rate of return for the project, measured as a percentage. In other words, the IRR is that interest rate which makes the present value of costs equal to the present value of benefits. Therefore, an IRR of .22 means that you expect the project to return an average of 22 percent per time period (usually measured in years). The higher the IRR, the better the project's return to the organization.

Payback Period

The payback period is defined as the number of time periods up to the point where cumulative revenues exceed cumulative costs, and therefore the project has finally "turned a profit" When comparing two or more projects, the shortest payback period identifies the project that becomes profitable most quickly. However, the payback period does not identify the expected magnitude of the total profit

Opportunity Cost

Opportunity cost is the cost of choosing one alternative and, therefore, giving up the potential benefits of another alternative. The understanding of opportunity cost causes management to treat project selection seriously because the organization is committing valuable, finite resources through decisions that often cannot be changed easily in the short run. Poor project selection may cause the company to miss out on better opportunities.

Sunk Cost

Sunk costs are expended costs over which we no longer have control; they are "water over the dam." The money is already spent, and you cannot have it back. Financial analysts have long professed that sunk costs should be ignored when making decisions about whether to continue investing in a project that is under way.

Constrained Optimization Methods

These methods include a variety of mathematical programming models that are used less often than other methods because they are more difficult to understand and use. Several examples follow.

- Linear and nonlinear programming
- Integer programming
- Dynamic programming
- Multiobjective programming
- Decision trees
- Forced choice
- Analytic hierarchy process

- Logical framework analysis

As a result, when organizations apply complex project selection criteria in a sophisticated model, it may be beneficial to treat the use of this model as a separate project phase.

It is not likely that you will encounter more than a question or two on this topic.

Scope Planning

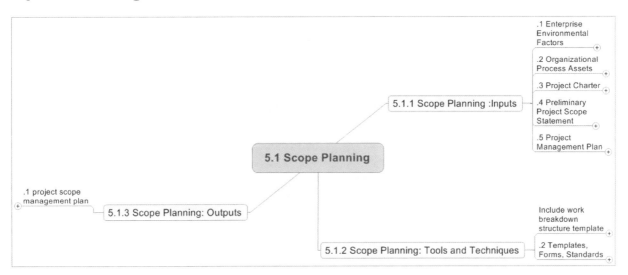

Scope planning is the process during which the scope statement is prepared. You should recognize the importance of the scope statement because it serves as the basis for future project decisions and includes the criteria to determine whether the entire project or a particular phase of the project has been completed successfully. Furthermore, the scope statement forms the basis for an agreement between the project team and the customer by identifying the project objectives and deliverables.

Tools and techniques for scope planning include product analysis and benefit/cost analysis (see earlier discussion of benefit-cost ratio under benefit measurement methods). Product analysis is used to develop a better understanding of the project's product. You should be familiar with some of the product analysis techniques:

- **Product breakdown analysis engineering**: Involves developing a better understanding of the product by breaking it down into constituent parts.

- **Value engineering**: Examines each element of a product or system to determine whether there is a more effective and less expensive way to achieve the same function.

- **Value analysis**: Focuses on optimizing cost performance. Systematic use of techniques to identify the required functions of an item, establish values for those functions, and provide the functions at the lowest overall cost without loss of performance.

- **Function analysis**: Examines the project's high-level requirements statements, identifying specific functions and estimating total costs based on the number of functions to be performed.

- **Quality function deployment (QFD)**: A customer-driven planning tool that guides the design, manufacturing, and marketing of goods. Every decision is made to meet the expressed needs of customers. A set of matrices is developed to relate the voice of the customer to the product's technical requirements, component requirements, process control plans, and manufacturing operations. These matrices comprise the House of Quality (a term that originated in 1972 at Mitsubishi's Kobe shipyard).

PMBOK® strongly recommends a written scope statement even if its elements have been included in other documents, such as the project charter. Elements that comprise the scope statement (enterprise environmental factors, organizational process assets, project charter, preliminary project scope statement, project management plan) are discussed in PMBOK® Para. 5.1.1.

PMBOK® Para. 5.1.3 also recommends that a scope management plan be prepared. The scope management plan should include a clear description of how scope changes will be identified and classified. This is particularly difficult, but it is absolutely essential when the product characteristics are still being elaborated. This may be a stand-alone document, or it may be part of the project plan.

Scope Definition

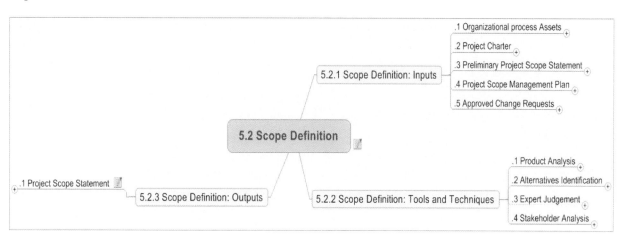

Scope definition is the subdivision of project deliverables into smaller (and more manageable) pieces until you have adequately identified in the work breakdown structure all the work on the project (PMBOK® Para. 5.2). In this way, adequate definition of the project scope provides the following three advantages:

1. Improved accuracy of cost, time, and resource estimates
2. A baseline for measuring progress and exercising control
3. Clear assignment of responsibility for project tasks

Thus, PMI® views proper scope definition as essential for project success.

Create Work Breakdown Structure (WBS)

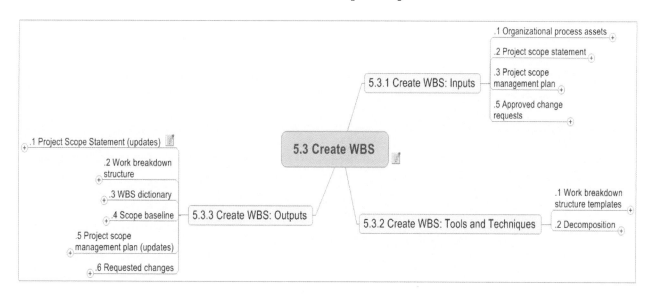

Work Breakdown Structure (WBS)

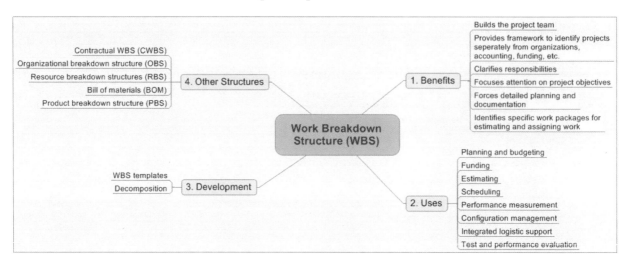

The WBS is the heart of the project planning effort. It is more than just an element of the project plan; it is the framework on which the project is built. No realistic overall project plan is possible without first developing a WBS that is detailed enough to provide meaningful identification of all project tasks that must be accomplished. The process of creating the WBS is very important, because during the process of breaking down the project, the project manager, the staff, and all involved functional managers are forced to think through all aspects of the project.

A WBS is a technique for breaking down a project into its component elements. It is a graphic picture of the hierarchy of the project (Figure 2-2), broken down level by level into subprojects and finally into tasks. It organizes the project by defining all the tasks that must be performed in the conception, design, development, fabrication, and test of the project hardware, software, or service. As the levels become lower, the scope, complexity, and cost of each subproject become smaller, until tasks that are completely capable of accomplishment are reached. These smallest tasks, called work packages, must be identified as manageable units that can be planned, budgeted, scheduled, and controlled. Work component descriptions often are collected in a WBS dictionary that will include work package descriptions as well as planning information, such as schedule dates, cost budgets, and staff assignments. The WBS indicates the relationship of the organizational structure to the project objectives and tasks, and so provides a firm basis for planning and controlling the project.

There are no hard-and-fast rules for preparing a WBS; good judgment is the only criterion. However, the size of these work packages is very important because they must be small enough in terms of cost and labor to permit realistic estimates to be made, and to simplify control. Many believe that the "80-hour rule can be of tremendous help in formulating the WBS and keeping it under control. This rule states that each task should be broken down into work packages that require no more than 80 hours of work for completion. At the end of each 80-hour-or-less period, the work package is reported simply as either completed or not completed. By means of such periodic check-ins, drifting of a project can be controlled early" (Stuckenbruck, The Implementation of Project Management). Other writers have mentioned the use of other "rules" for work package durations. However, PMI® has used the 80-hour rule in its exam for many years. So be on the lookout for it.

Benefits of Using a WBS

- Builds the project team

- Provides a framework to identify projects separately from organizations, accounting systems, funding sources, and so on

- Clarifies responsibilities

- Focuses attention on project objectives Forces detailed planning and documentation

- Identifies specific work packages for estimating and assigning work

Uses of the WBS

- Planning and budgeting
- Funding
- Estimating
- Scheduling
- Performance measurement
- Configuration management
- Integrated logistic support
- Test and performance evaluation

Development of the WBS

- WBS templates

- Decomposition: This requires subdividing the major project deliverables into smaller, more manageable components by—

  - Identifying the major deliverables of the project, including project management

  - Deciding whether adequate cost and duration estimates can be developed in sufficient detail for each deliverable. If not, then identify constituent components of the deliverable in terms of tangible, verifiable results. When adequate detail exists, the last step is to verify the correctness of the breakdown. To do this, you need to determine whether—

    - The lower-level items are both necessary and sufficient for the broken down item

    - Each item is clearly and completely defined

    - Each item can be appropriately scheduled, budgeted, and assigned to an organizational unit

Other Structures

Do not confuse the WBS with other types of "breakdown" structures, such as the—

- ***Contractual WBS (CWBS)***: Used to define the level of reporting that the seller will provide the buyer

- ***Organizational breakdown structure (OBS)***: Used to depict which organizational units are responsible for certain work components

- ***Resource breakdown structure (RBS), a variant of the OBS***: Used to define when work components are assigned to individuals

- ***Bill of materials (BOM)***: Used to present a hierarchical view of the physical assemblies, subassemblies, and components needed to fabricate a manufactured product

- ***Product breakdown structure, (PBS), virtually similar to the WBS***: Used in other application areas when the term IIWBS" is used incorrectly to refer to a BOM

Scope Verification

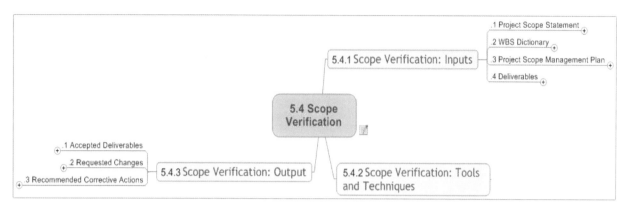

Scope verification is the process of formalizing acceptance of the project scope by the stakeholders. It requires reviewing work products and results to ensure that all were completed correctly and satisfactorily, and preparing and distributing documentation indicating that the client or sponsor has accepted the product of the project. Scope verification differs from quality control, although both are controlling processes. Scope verification is primarily concerned with acceptance of work results, whereas quality control is concerned with correctness of work results. These processes should be performed in parallel.

Inspection is the tool and technique used for scope verification and involves activities, such as measuring, examining, and testing that are undertaken to determine whether results conform to requirements. You should be familiar with terms that could be used for inspections, including reviews, product reviews, audits, and walkthroughs.

Formal acceptance is the output from scope verification. It is documentation that the client or the sponsor has accepted the product of the project, phase, or major deliverable. Recognize that this acceptance may be conditional, especially at the end of a phase.

Risk and Complexity Trade-offs

Risk and uncertainty are covered extensively in Unit 8. However, there is one facet of the complexity and risk trade-off that has particular relevance to scope management. Consider the following question:

As complexity on your project increases, the level of risk or uncertainty in attempting to define the scope of the work is likely to—

a. Decrease
b. Increase
c. Remain the same

The correct answer is "b."

Scope Control

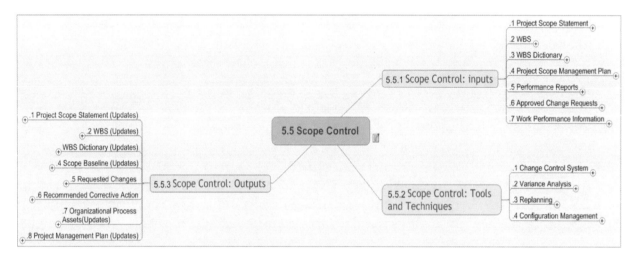

Scope control covers issues similar to integrated change control, but it focuses solely on scope changes. You should recognize that scope change requests may occur in different forms and may come from different sources:

- Oral or written
- Direct or indirect
- Externally or internally initiated
- Legally mandated or optional

NOTE: These changes may either expand the project's scope or contract it. Changes are generally the result of—

- An external event

- An error or omission when the scope of the product or project was initially designed

- A value-added change

- Implementing a contingency plan or a workaround plan

A scope change is described (PMBOK® Para. 4.4.1.4) as any modification to the agreed-upon scope as defined by the approved WBS. You should be aware that scope changes might lead to and require changes in cost, time, quality, or other project objectives. However, only project scope changes affect the performance measurement baseline. Depending on the nature of the change, the corresponding baseline document may be revised and reissued to reflect the approved change and form the new baseline for future changes. This is known as the adjusted baseline.

Practice Questions

INSTRUCTIONS: Note the most suitable answer for each multiple-choice question in the appropriate space on the answer sheet.

1. You are working on a product development project under contract to an automotive company that is building the "next-millennium Yugo." Initially, the product was defined as "a state-of-the-art personal transportation vehicle." Later it was described as "a state-of-the-art personal transportation vehicle that requires no gasoline." Finally, after an all-night hot tub party with the design engineers, it was described as "a state-of-the-art personal transportation vehicle that requires no gasoline, costs less than USD $15,000, and does not make any noise." This shows the progressive elaboration of product characteristics. But, although the product characteristics are elaborated progressively, they must be coordinated carefully with the—

   a. Proper project scope definition
   b. Project stakeholders
   c. Scope control system
   d. Customer's strategic plan

2. Last week you were lying on the beach in Key West. Today you are examining a pile of scope change requests on a project you were asked to take over because the previous project manager decided to resign and open a catfish farm in Arkansas. To assess the degree to which the project scope will change, you need to compare the requests to which project document?

   a. Scope statement
   b. WBS
   c. Project plan
   d. Scope management plan

3. Your company's project review committee (PRC) meets quarterly to review any project with a budget exceeding $2 million. You recently were promoted to senior project manager and was assigned one of these large projects, the development of a next-generation, computer-aided manufacturing process. The PRC asked you to present the project's objectives, work content, and deliverables at its next meeting. Accordingly, you need to prepare which one of the following documents—

   a. Project charter

b. Product description
c. Scope statement
d. WBS

4. Your company, a leading pharmaceutical firm, has more project opportunities to pursue than resources available to complete them. You are leading a team to establish a project selection and prioritization method. The team is considering many different management concerns, including financial return, market share, and public perception. You told the team that the most important of the various criteria for building a project selection model is—

   a. Capability
   b. Realism
   c. Ease of use
   d. Cost

5. Thinking back to the lessons your company learned from its experiences with its legacy information systems during the Y2K dilemma, you finally convinced management to consider systems maintenance from the beginning of the project. However, regardless of what design considerations are factored into the project, maintenance should—

   a. Always be included as an activity to be performed during the closeout phase
   b. Have a separate phase in the life cycle for information systems projects because 60% to 70% of computer systems' life cycle costs generally are devoted to maintenance
   c. Not be viewed as part of the project life cycle
   d. Be viewed as a separate project

6. You are beginning a new project staffed with a virtual team that is located in five countries. Based on experience, you recognize that team members in a matrix environment sometimes will be more responsive to their functional managers than to you, their project manager. Anticipating conflict in work priorities among your team, you ask the project sponsor to prepare a—

   a. Memo to team members informing them that they work for you now
   b. Project charter
   c. Memo to the functional managers informing them that you have authority to direct their employees
   d. Human resource management plan

7. A project is an ideal environment in which to use the management-by-objectives technique because—

   a. Project management involves setting organizational objectives
   b. Projects generally are handled through a matrix management environment
   c. Project managers' responsibilities are defined in terms of corporate objectives
   d. All projects should be strongly oriented toward goals and objectives

8. Your company, Nutritional Chickens, is embarking on a project to completely eliminate the threat of salmonella in its products. You are the project manager for this project, and you have just finished the concept phase. The deliverable for this phase is the—

   a. Project plan
   b. Statement of work
   c. Project charter
   d. Resource spreadsheet

9. A senior partner with the prestigious firm, Milkem & Fleecem, Inc., asked you to help a key client decide which project selection method to use. The client's company engineers are convinced that constrained optimization methods will work best; however, the sales staff believes that benefit measurement methods are better (and the math is easier!). You have just graduated with a degree in large animal science, and you are unfamiliar with this specific issue. The client is paying Milkem & Fleecem $2,000 a day for your advice, however, so you must say something intelligent at the next meeting. You drag out the PMBOK® and prepare a slick presentation enumerating the pros and cons of each method. You conclude your presentation with a quiz that reads: All the following are examples of constrained optimization methods except—

   a. Analytic hierarchy process
   b. Logical framework analysis
   c. Economic model
   d. Multi-objective programming

10. Rather than use a WBS as you suggested, your team developed a bill of materials to define the project's work components. A customer review of this document uncovered that a scope change was needed, and a change request was subsequently written. This is an example of a change request that was the result of—

    a. An external event

    b. An error or omission in defining the scope of the product

    c. A value-adding change

    d. An error or omission in defining the scope of the project

11. When selecting a project, it is always important to measure value or attractiveness to the project owner. Your company uses multiple criteria for project selection but combines them into a single value function. You also have established a way to determine value under uncertainty. This is known as the—

    a. Choice of alternative methods to perform the project

    b. Decision model and calculation method

    c. Logical framework analysis

    d. Analytic hierarchy process

12. You have prepared the scope statement and the WBS for your project. You also have an approved project plan. Your project is now under way, but you recognize that, given the nature of project work, scope change is inevitable. You also are aware of the danger of scope creep, having suffered the consequences of it recently. To avoid a similar experience, you meet with your team and decide to establish a project scope control system. This is—

    a. A collection of formal, documented procedures to define the steps by which official project documents may be changed

    b. A documented process used to apply technical and administrative direction and surveillance to identify and document functional and physical characteristics of items, record and report change, control change, and audit the items and system to verify conformance to requirements

    c. A set of procedures by which project scope may be changed, including the paperwork, tracking systems, and approval levels necessary for authorizing change

    d. Mandatory for use on projects so that the scope management plan cannot be changed without prior review and sign-off

13. Because you were a finance major in college, you have been asked to be an active participant in your company's project selection process. The project selection committee chair has asked you to describe ground rules and possible approaches for project selection. You know that organizations usually will not approve a project if its costs exceed its benefits, so you recommend using a discounted cash-flow approach. This approach is based in part on the economic theory that a dollar today generally is worth more than a dollar a year from now. Using this approach, the project is acceptable if the—

   a.   Sum of the net present value of all estimated cash flow during the life of the project equals the profit
   b.   Net present value of the inflow is greater than the net present value of the outflow by a specified amount or percentage
   c.   Gross present value of all future expected cash flow divided by the initial cash investment is greater than one
   d.   Payback period occurs by the second year of the project

14. You want to structure your project so that each project team member has a discrete work package to perform. The work package is a—

   a. Deliverable at the lowest level of the WBS
   b. Task with a unique identifier
   c. Required level of reporting
   d. Task that can be assigned to more than one organizational unit

15. You are project manager for a systems integration effort that will allow the public to purchase lottery tickets in hospital emergency rooms throughout the province. Your firm is developing the software for the application, but you need to procure the hardware components from external sources. Your subcontracts administrator has told you to prepare a product description, which in this case is also called a—

   a.   Statement of work
   b.   Contract scope statement
   c.   Project charter
   d.   Contract

16. You recently joined a state agency after working in private industry for 10 years. Your previous employer, a defense contractor, had a detailed project management methodology requiring multiple in-progress reviews. Although project management is fairly new to the state agency, it has a project life cycle with four phases: concept, definition, execution, and finish. Although the agency's project life cycle does not mandate when or how many project reviews should be conducted, you believe it is important to review project performance at the conclusion of each project phase. The objective of such a review is to—

   a. Determine how many resources are required to complete the project according to the project baseline
   b. Adjust the schedule and cost baselines based on past performance

    c. Obtain customer acceptance of project deliverables

    d. Determine whether the project should continue to the next phase

17. Your customer signed off on the requirements definition document and scope statement of your video game project last month. Today she requested a project scope change. She would like to make it an interactive game that can be played on a person's television and on a computer. This represents a scope change that, at a minimum—

    a. Modifies the project's agreed-upon scope as defined by the WBS

    b. Results in a change to all project baselines

    c. Requires adjustments to cost, time, quality, and other objectives

    d. Results in a lesson learned

18. You are lying in bed, listening to the air-conditioning system pump lukewarm air into your motel room. You are dreading the next day because you must face an extremely tough client. Suddenly, the phone rings: it is your senior partner from Milkem & Fleecem, Inc. He is pulling you off your current project and has assigned you to another project. Based on your project management experience, you know that, ideally, a project manager should be selected and assigned—

    a. During the initiating process

    b. During the project planning process

    c. At the end of the concept phase of the project life cycle

    d. Prior to the beginning of the development phase of the project life cycle

19. Because of a new government regulation, you had to change the scope of your telecommunications project. Several changes were made to the project's objectives. You have updated the project's technical and planning documents as needed. Your next step should be to—

    a. Notify stakeholders as appropriate

    b. Revise the company's knowledge management system

    c. Obtain formal acceptance from your sponsor and customer

    d. Prepare a performance report

20. During the concept phase of your project, management indicated that it wants the expected benefit of each new product to outweigh its development costs. This is an example of—

    a. An assumption

  b. A constraint

  c. Use of the constrained-optimization method of project selection

  d. A technical requirement

21. You have been appointed project manager for a new project in your organization and must prepare a project plan. To help you provide the framework for this project, you decide to prepare a WBS to show the magnitude and complexity of the work involved. No WBS templates are available to help you. To prepare the WBS, your first step should be to—

  a. Determine the cost and duration estimates for each project deliverable

  b. Identify the major project deliverables

  c. Identify the components of each project deliverable

  d. Determine the key tasks to be performed

22. You are a personnel management specialist for the human resources department. You recently were assigned to a new project team. The team is working on a project to establish a team-based reward and recognition system for all company projects that last more than 1 year and that have some team members committed to work on the project at least half-time. The other team members also work in the human resources department. The project charter should be issued by—

  a. The project manager

  b. The head of the human resources department

  c. A manager external to the project

  d. A member of the program management office (PMO) who has jurisdiction over human resources

23. Your company, HealthNut, Inc., is a leading marketer of dietary supplements that can be produced quickly and without regulatory approval. Management wants to explore new markets and new products to boost revenue and profits. You are leading a team to identify potential products. Because of your background and interest in information technology, you recommended developing wireless communications products. But when you submitted the idea for review, executive management informed you that this product would not fit with the organization's core competencies. You need to go back to the drawing board and recommend other products using management's guideline as—

  a. An assumption

  b. A risk

c. A specification
d. A technical requirement

24. The U.S. Bureau of Indian Affairs awarded your firm a contract to renovate an elementary school on a Navajo reservation. One contractual term, Indian preference, requires you to hire Native American laborers and subcontractors from the reservation. This is an example of which type of the following constraints?

a. Social
b. Economical
c. Environmental
d. Legal

25. Historical information is used—

a. To compare current performance with prospective lessons learned
b. To prepare the stakeholder management plan
c. To evaluate the skills and competencies of prospective team members
d. As an input to project initiation

26. Your organization's research department has isolated an advanced microbe that, when combined with seaweed, can be formulated into a biodegradable composite material. The sales department believes such a material should be used to produce socks that can be worn once then used as garden fertilizer. Management asked you to determine whether a project should be initiated to produce this line of clothing. Accordingly, you need to prepare a—

a. Feasibility study
b. Return on investment report
c. Make-or-buy analysis
d. Project charter

27. On an environmental remediation project, an example of a value-adding change is a change that—

a. Is caused by a new or revised government regulation, necessitating that the design be resubmitted
b. Takes advantage of cost-reducing technology that was not available when the scope originally was defined
c. Uses a bill of materials to define the scope of the project, including all assemblies and subassemblies

    d. Corrects omission of a required feature in the design of a system

28. The greatest degree of uncertainty is encountered during which phase of the project life cycle?

    a. Concept
    b. Planning
    c. Implementation
    d. Closeout

29. Scope verification—

    a. Improves cost and schedule accuracy, particularly on projects using innovative techniques or technology
    b. Is the last activity performed on a project before handoff to the customer
    c. Documents the characteristics of the product or service that the project was undertaken to create
    d. Differs from quality control in that scope verification is concerned with the acceptance-not the correctness-of the work results

30. Specifying the project's technical requirements is an important step because such requirements—

    a. Describe the characteristics of the deliverable in ordinary language
    b. Are used by the project staff to target efforts
    c. Are useful to both the project staff and the customers
    d. Are designed to ensure that customers know what they are getting from a project

31. You have been placed in charge of a group of people that is selecting one of three possible projects. The project is to develop an antidote to prickly heat. As you gather in the conference room, many of the team members already have decided which project selection technique to use. Some prefer IRR, and others argue for BCR. In deciding which method to use, your first step should be to—

    a. Compare and contrast selection techniques, and identify the advantages and disadvantages of each
    b. Identify the technique used most often in the company and determine if it is appropriate for this project
    c. Select the method that most team members are knowledgeable of
    d. Determine the philosophy and wishes of management

32. Written change orders should be required on—

    a. All projects, large and small
    b. Only large projects
    c. Projects with a formal configuration management system in place
    d. Projects for which the cost of a change control system can be justified

33. Your company, a conference management firm, is branching out into new areas. As a result, it responded to a government agency's request for proposals for historical research. Your company won the bid, and you are the project manager for its first historical research project. Unfortunately, your work products do not meet government standards for historical research. The company president just received formal notification from the agency's contracting officer that, as a result, it would terminate the project for convenience. Now you must—

    a. Submit the work products to date to your contracting officer's technical representative
    b. Document lessons learned and index the records
    c. Establish and document the level and extent of completion
    d. Shut down the project office and reassign all personnel

34. The principal sources of project failure are—

    a. Lack of a projectized or strong matrix structure, poor scope definition, and lack of a project plan
    b. Lack of commitment or support by top management, disharmony on the project team, and lack of leadership by the project manager
    c. Poorly identified customer needs, a geographically dispersed project team, and little communication with the customer until the project is delivered
    d. Organizational factors, poorly identified customer needs, inadequately specified project requirements, and poor planning and control

35. The project management plan is important in change control because it—

    a. Provides the baseline against which changes are managed
    b. Provides information on project performance

    c. Alerts the project team to issues that may cause problems in the future
    d. Is expected to change throughout the project

36. You are the project manager for a major company project. You recently assigned a scope of work to a subcontractor. The subcontractor needs to plan and manage that specific scope of work in a more detailed manner. Your friend Michele is the new project manager for the subcontractor. She also is new to the project management profession. You suggest that she first—

a. Follow the WBS that you developed for the project and use the work packages you identified
b. Develop a subproject WBS for the work package that is her company's responsibility
c. Establish a similar coding structure to facilitate use of a common project management information system
d. Develop a WBS dictionary to show specific staff assignments

37. Your technical team leader has prepared a request for a value-adding change on your project that will result in expanding the project scope. To help assess the magnitude of any variations as the work to implement the change proceeds, you have mandated that earned value analysis be used. This approach represents a—

a. Performance measurement technique
b. Configuration management process
c. Cost accounting procedure
d. Scope reporting mechanism

38. You are working in the pharmaceutical industry. Your project has been defined as clinical trials for the drug Fantastica, which improves human memory and stimulates hair growth. As the project proceeds, the product is described more explicitly as four Phase I trials, five Phase II trials, and six Phase III trials. This situation provides an example of—

a. Quality function deployment
b. Close alignment of project activities with the WBS
c. Value analysis
d. Progressive elaboration of the product description

39. Project success depends on a number of interrelated factors, including time, cost, and scope control. However, the success of any project depends primarily on—

a. Customer acceptance

b. Customer satisfaction
c. Customer compromise in defining its needs
d. Exceeding customer requirements through gold-plating

40. You are establishing a PMO for the National Animal Celebrity Management Program, which consists of 15 separate projects. The PMO will have a project management information system. This system will be an on-line repository of all program data. You will collect descriptions of all work components for each of the 15 projects. This information will form an integral part of the—

a. Chart of accounts
b. WBS dictionary
c. WBS structure template
d. Earned value management reports

Answer Sheet

Answer Key

1. a. **Proper project scope definition**

    Progressive elaboration of product characteristics must be coordinated carefully with proper scope definition, particularly when the project is performed under contract. When properly defined, the project scope--the work to be done-- should remain constant even when the product characteristics are elaborated progressively. [Planning]

    PMI®, PMBOK®, 2004, 6

2. b. **WBS**

    The WBS defines the project's scope baseline, which provides the basis for any changes that may occur on the project. [Planning]

    PMI®, PMBOK®, 2004, 112

3. c. **Scope statement**

    The scope statement provides stakeholders with a common understanding of the scope of the project and is a source of reference for making future project decisions. [Planning]

    PMI®, PMBOK®, 2004, 86

4. b. **Realism**

    The model should reflect the objectives of the company and its managers; consider the realities of the organization's limitations on facilities, capital, and personnel; and include factors for risk-the technical risks of performance, cost, and time and the market risk of customer rejection. [Initiating]

    Meredith and Mantel 2000, 4-12

5. c. **Not be viewed as part of the project life cycle**

    Projects are efforts that occur within a finite period of time with clearly defined beginnings and ends. Maintenance is ongoing and of an indefinite duration. A maintenance activity, such as revision of an organization's purchasing guidelines, may be viewed as a project but is a separate and distinct undertaking from the initial project that generated it. [Initiating]

Frame 1995, 16

6.   b. Project charter

Although the project charter cannot stop conflicts from arising, it can provide a framework to help resolve them because it describes the project manager's authority to apply organizational resources to project activities. [Initiating]

Meredith and Mantel 2000, 238

7.   d.   All projects should be strongly oriented toward goals and objectives

Management by objectives focuses on the goals of an activity rather than on the activity itself, so managers are held responsible for obtaining results rather than performing certain activities. These results can be used to help evaluate project performance. [Initiating]

Stuckenbruck 1981, 157

8.   c.   Project charter

This document signifies official sanction by top management and starts the planning, or development, phase. The project charter formally recognizes the existence of the project and provides the project manager with the authority to apply organizational resources to project activities. [Initiating]

PMI®, PMBOK®, 2004, 81

9.   c. Economic model

Economic models include benefit measurement methods, along with comparative approaches, scoring models, and benefit contribution. [Initiating]

PMI®, PMBOK®, 2004, 54

10. d. An error or omission in defining the scope of the project

The bill of materials presents a hierarchical view of the physical assemblies, subassemblies, and components needed to fabricate a manufactured product, whereas the WBS is a deliverable-oriented
grouping of project components used to define the total scope of the project. Using a bill of materials where a WBS would be more appropriate may result in an ill-defined scope and subsequent change requests. [Controlling]

PMI®, PMBOK®, 2004, 112

11. b. Decision model and calculation method

Use of a decision criterion is one part of project selection. If multiple criteria are used, the criteria should be combined into a single value function and a means of calculating value under uncertainty. This is known as the decision model and calculation method. [Initiating]

PMI®, PMBOK®, 2004, 54

12. c. A set of procedures by which project scope may be changed, including the paperwork, tracking systems, and approval levels necessary for authorizing change

In addition to complying with any relevant contractual provisions, scope control must be integrated with the project's overall change control system and with any systems in place to control project and product scope. [Controlling]

PMI®, PMBOK®, 2004, 119

13. b. Net present value of the inflow is greater than the net present value of the outflow by a specified amount or percentage

The discounted cash-flow approach--or the present value method-- determines the net present value of all cash flow by discounting it by the required rate of return. The impact of inflation can be considered. Early in the life of a. project, net cash flow is likely to be negative because the major outflow is the initial investment in the project. If the project is successful, cash flow will become positive. [Initiating]

Meredith and Mantel 2000, 48-49

14. a. Deliverable at the lowest level of the WBS

A work package is the lowest or smallest unit of work division in a project or WBS. Typically, a work package contains about 80 hours of work. [Planning]

PMI®, PMBOK®, 2004, 113 and 114

15. a. Statement of work

Many projects involve one organization (the seller) doing work under contract to another (the buyer). In such circumstances, the buyer provides the initial product description, which is also called a statement of work. [Initiating]

PMI®, PMBOK®, 2004, 82

16. d. Determine whether the project should continue to the next phase

The review at the end is called a phase exit; stage gate, or kill point. The purpose of this review is to determine whether the project should continue to the next phase, to detect and correct errors while they are still manageable, and to ensure that the project remains focused on the business need it was undertaken to address. [Initiating]

PMI®, PMBOK®, 2004, 44

17. a. Modifies the project's agreed-upon scope as defined by the WBS

A scope change is an output of overall scope control. Although a scope change may require adjustments to other project baselines and objectives, such assessments are made on a case-by-case basis. [Controlling]

PMI®, PMBOK®, 2004, 119

18. a. During the initiating process

If the project manager is selected and assigned to the project during initiation, several of the usual start-up tasks of the project are simplified. In addition, becoming involved with project activities from the beginning helps the project manager understand where the project fits within the organization in terms of its priority relative to other projects and the ongoing work of the organization. [Initiating]

Meredith and Mantel 2000, 85

19. a. Notify stakeholders as appropriate

Scope changes are fed back through the planning process and may require modifications to cost, time, quality, or other project objectives. Once technical and planning documents are updated, stakeholders should be notified. [Controlling]

PMI®, PMBOK®, 2004, 121

20. b. A constraint

Constraints are factors that will limit the team's options. [Initiating]

PMI®, PMBOK®, 2004, 354

21. b. Identify the major project deliverables

This is the first step in the decomposition of a project. The deliverables should be defined in terms of how the project will be organized. For example, the phases of the project life cycle may be used as the first level of decomposition with the project deliverables repeated at the second level. [Planning]

PMI®, PMBOK®, 2004, 114

22. c. A manager external to the project

The project charter should be issued by a manager outside the project but at a level appropriate to the project's needs. Because it provides the project manager with the authority to apply organizational resources to project activities, the project charter should not be issued by the project manager. Functional managers should have approval authority. [Initiating]

PMI®, PMBOK®, 2004, 81

23. a. An assumption

Assumptions are factors that, for planning purposes, are considered to be true, real, or certain. They are an output of the initiating process and are an input into scope planning. [Initiating]

PMI®, PMBOK®, 2004, 352

24. d. Legal

The terms and conditions in any contract are legal requirements that must be adhered to by the parties entering into the agreement. [Initiating]

PMI®, PMBOK®, 2004, 65

25. d. As an input to project initiation

Reviewing past projects often helps a person prepare cost and schedule estimates and a risk management plan for the current project. [Initiating]

PMI®, PMBOK®, 2004, 51

26.   a.   Feasibility study

Such a study attempts to explain whether the project can be successfully completed, based on resources required, schedule limitations, budget constraints, and any other factors that could impede the organization's efforts. [Initiating]

PMI®, PMBOK®, 2004, 43

27. b. Takes advantage of cost-reducing technology that was not available when the scope was originally defined

Most changes are the result of external events or errors or omissions in scope definition, or they are value-adding, that is, they add value to the project while reducing costs. [Controlling]

PMI®, PMBOK®, 2004, 119

28. a. Concept

The greatest degree of uncertainty about the future is encountered during the concept phase. The direction of the project is determined in this phase, and the decisions made have the greatest influence on scope, quality, time, and cost of the project. [Initiating]

Wideman 1992, 11-1

29. d. Differs from quality control in that scope verification is concerned with the acceptance--not the correctness--of the work results

The output from scope verification is documentation that the customer has accepted the project product. [Controlling]

PMI®, PMBOK®, 2004, 118

30. b. Are used by the project staff to target efforts

To develop the project plan, needs are formulated as functional requirements. Technical requirements emerge from the functional requirements because the latter generally do not offer enough precise guidance to project staff. [Planning]

Frame 1995,116-117

31. d. Determine the philosophy and wishes of management

Any selection technique must be evaluated based on the degree to which it will meet the organization's objective for the project. Management generally establishes the organization's objective. Therefore, management's wishes must be identified first. Then the most appropriate model to support management's wishes should be selected. [Initiating]

Meredith and Mantel 2000, 43

32. a. All projects, large and small

A system is needed for careful monitoring of changes made to the requirements. Use of written change orders encourages the individuals asking for changes to take responsibility for their requests and reduces frivolous requests that may adversely affect the project. [Controlling]

Frame 1995, 153

33. c. Establish and document the level and extent of completion

The scope verification process involves obtaining stakeholders' formal acceptance of project scope. If a project is terminated before it is complete, the level and extent of completion should be established and documented. [Controlling]

PMI®, PMBOK®, 2004, 118

34. d. Organizational factors, poorly identified customer needs, inadequately specified project requirements, and poor planning and control

Organizational problems, such as separation of responsibility and authority, can hinder the work being done and lead to poor quality; poorly identified customer needs and inadequately specified project requirements can result in a product that is unusable or grossly underused; and poor planning and control can create a chaotic environment and poor project results. [Initiating]

Frame 1995, 19-22

35. a. Provides the baseline against which changes are managed

The project management plan is a key input to integrated change control. [Controlling]

PMI®, PMBOK®, 2004, 96

36. b. Develop a subproject WBS for the work package that is her company's responsibility

Work packages are items at the lowest level of the WBS. A subproject WBS breaks down work packages into greater detail. A subproject WBS generally is used if the project manager assigns a scope of work to another organization, and the project manager at that organization must plan and manage the scope of work in greater detail. [Planning]

PMI®, PMBOK®, 2004, 113-114

37. a. Performance measurement technique

Performance measurement techniques, such as variance analysis, trend analysis, earned value analysis, and performance reviews, help assess the magnitude of any variations that may occur in project performance so that the cause of the variances can be determined and corrective action be taken if needed. [Controlling]

PMI®, PMBOK®, 2004, 266

38. d. Progressive elaboration of the product description

The product description documents the characteristics of the product or service that the project was undertaken to create. This description will generally have less detail in early phases and more detail in later ones as the product characteristics are elaborated progressively. [Initiating]

PMI®, PMBOK®, 2004, 6

39. b. Customer satisfaction

Customer satisfaction, not time or cost, is the primary criterion for measuring project success. [Initiating]

Frame 1994, 106-109

40. b . WBS dictionary

The WBS dictionary typically includes work package descriptions and other planning information such as schedule dates, cost budgets, and staff assignments. [Planning]

PMI®, PMBOK®, 2004, 379

Notes

Notes

Notes

Notes

Notes

Mind Mapped Notes

Mind Mapped Notes

Mind Mapped Notes

Get the entire series of PMP® Certification Exam Study Guides today at www.LighthouseBookseller.com!

Professional Responsibility

Project Communications Management

Project Cost Management

Project Human Resource Management

Project Integration Management

Project Procurement Management

Project Quality Management

Project Risk Management

Project Scope Management

Project Time Management

Tips on Studying for and Taking the PMP ® Exam

Exercise Your Mind!

Sudoku for Project Managers

Sudoku for Business Analysts

Sudoku for Executives

Kakuro for Project Managers

Kakuro for Business Analysts

Kakuro for Executives

Our Sudoku and Kakuro puzzle books have bits of vital knowledge for Project Managers, Business Analysts, and Executives; all broken up by Sudoku or Kakuro puzzles. Visit www.LighthouseBookseller.com to get the entire series.

Made in the USA